SPORTS FAMILIES™

VENUS AND SERENA WILLIAMS

TENNIS CHAMPIONS

Diane Bailey

rosen publishing's
rosen
central®

New York

Published in 2010 by The Rosen Publishing Group, Inc.
29 East 21st Street, New York, NY 10010

Library of Congress Cataloging-in-Publication Data

Bailey, Diane, 1966–
Venus and Serena Williams: tennis champions / Diane Bailey.—1st ed.
    p. cm.—(Sports families)
Includes bibliographical references and index.
ISBN 978-1-4358-3552-8 (library binding)
ISBN 978-1-4358-8520-2 (pbk)
ISBN 978-1-4358-8521-9 (6 pack)
1. Williams, Venus, 1980-—Juvenile literature. 2. Williams, Serena, 1981-—Juvenile literature. 3. Tennis players—United States—Biography—Juvenile literature. 4. African American women tennis players—Biography—Juvenile literature. I. Title.
GV994.A1B35 2010
796.342092'2—dc22

[B]

2009015449

Manufactured in the United States of America

CPSIA Compliance Information: Batch #LW10YA: For Further Information contact Rosen Publishing, New York, New York at 1-800-237-9932

On the cover: Serena and Venus Williams holding their trophy after winning their eighth career Grand Slam women's doubles title at the Australian Open in 2009.

On the back cover: NASCAR is a registered trademark of the National Association for Stock Car Auto Racing, Inc.

Contents

For Venus *(right)* and Serena Williams, their relationship is more important than tennis. After they face one another at a tournament, the sisters take a few moments to congratulate—or console—each other.

For Venus Williams, the hard part is finished. It's March 1999, and she has just won the Lipton Championship tennis tournament in Key Biscayne, Florida.

Now she's in the car on her way to the awards ceremony. Her cell phone rings. Who could be calling? It's the woman Venus just beat.

What follows is not a polite conversation where the loser simply congratulates the winner. Hardly! The person on the other end of the phone isn't just Venus's opponent—it's her sister, Serena.

The match wasn't an easy win for Venus. It was the first one where the sisters played against each other in the finals. It was hard for Venus to beat her sister, but Serena doesn't hold any hard feelings. There are no grudges, just giggling together on the phone. The tennis match is over, and they're on to other things.

Look at the score of a tennis game between Venus and Serena Williams, and there will always be love. In tennis, "love" is another way to say someone's score is zero. But even if Venus and Serena both have points on the scoreboard, their love for each other is always there.

It may not be obvious. Venus won't put away her ace serve. Serena won't ease up on her killer backhand. Each woman is out there to win—even if it is against her own sister.

They have now met in the finals of every major tennis event in the world. Their Sister Slams—where they play each other—are big news in sports. Throughout their matches, they grunt and sweat, giving the most of their awesome athletic abilities. But no matter who wins, afterward they go back to just being sisters.

About a year before the Lipton Championship, in 1998, the two had met for the first time as pros at the Australian Open. Venus won. As they left the court, Venus said, "I'm sorry I had to take you out, Serena."

But she also knew that was her job—to compete the best she knew how. It's what helped her become great. It's what helped Serena become great. As the older sister, Venus paved the way for the two sisters to become tennis superstars. Without Serena, though, neither one of them would have become who they are. They needed each other. They still do. It is family that has made them great and family that will carry them into the next step of their lives.

Chapter One

SISTER ACT

In 1984, Venus Williams was only four years old. She was too young to be able to count to 500. But she could hit that many tennis balls!

Venus and her father, Richard, would fill a grocery shopping cart with tennis balls. They loaded the cart into the family car and then drove over to the public tennis courts.

The tennis courts were old and run-down. They often had to clear away garbage before they could play. But it was good enough for Venus. She loved tennis. Serena joined the family lessons a year later. She wanted to be just like her big sister. She loved tennis, too.

Venus was born on June 17, 1980. Her sister Serena was born on September 26, 1981. One day their father was watching TV. He saw a woman win a tennis tournament. She got a check for thousands of dollars. Richard thought his girls could do the same thing.

Richard didn't know anything about tennis. He'd never played the game. But that didn't stop him. He bought books and videos about how to play tennis. He and his wife, Oracene, learned how to play. Then they taught their daughters.

The Williams family lived in Compton, California. Compton is a town in southern Los Angeles. Unfortunately, there was a lot of crime in their neighborhood. Venus and Serena remember that people fired guns around them. Their father would yell, "Duck!"

As young girls, Venus *(left)* and Serena stand with their father, Richard Williams, who took an active role in their careers.

But Venus and Serena weren't scared off. They wanted to play tennis. Richard made a deal with the gang members who lived in the area. They guarded the courts while Venus and Serena practiced.

Venus and Serena had three older sisters, from Oracene's first marriage. But Yetunde, Isha, and Lyndrea didn't take to tennis like Venus and Serena did. In fact, Venus liked tennis so much that Richard once said he actually had to take her racket away sometimes. He wanted her to be good at tennis, but he didn't think she should like it too much. Richard and Oracene believed the most important things in life were their family, their religion (they are Jehovah's Witnesses), and their education. Tennis came after all that.

GETTING NOTICED

Soon Richard started entering Venus in tournaments. She won them all. When she was 10 years old, her record was 63–0. She was ranked number one in her age group. Richard liked to call his daughter the "Cinderella of the ghetto."

Venus had talent. People started to notice, not only in California, but across the country. The *New York Times* ran an article about Venus. The headline read: "Status: Undefeated. Future: Rosy. Age: 10."

Richard agreed that Venus's future was rosy. He also believed she needed a change. He had worked with Venus up to this point, but now she was good enough that she needed a professional coach. Richard contacted a tennis coach in Florida. His name was Rick Macci.

Macci traveled to California to play tennis with Venus. He hit a few balls with her. He didn't think she was all that great. Then Venus took a bathroom break. Macci watched her walk 10 yards (9 meters) on her hands and then do cartwheels for another 10 yards. Macci told *Tennis* magazine that now he was impressed. "The first thing I thought was, 'I've got a female Michael Jordan on my hands,'" he said.

In tennis, players usually start on the junior circuit. They play with other children, near their age, with a similar skill level. This is where Venus and Serena started. But they didn't last long.

After moving to Florida, Venus worked with professional coach Rick Macci.

Serena won almost all of her matches, too. Richard thought his daughters needed a different challenge. He worried they wouldn't thrive if they stayed on the junior circuit. For one thing, they were better than anyone else they played. But there was more. Richard thought a lot of the other parents put too much pressure on their children. He didn't want his daughters to burn out and end up hating the game they loved.

Richard may also have been worried that the girls would face racism. Historically, most tennis players have been Caucasian (white). Venus and Serena are black. Only a handful of African American players have succeeded professionally in tennis.

Richard decided to pull Venus and Serena off the junior circuit. Some people thought this was a bad decision. Most professional players learn on the junior circuit before going pro. Richard ignored them. For his daughters, he said, training on their own was the best course.

PRACTICE, PRACTICE, PRACTICE

In 1991, the Williams family moved to Florida. There, Venus and Serena could be taught by trained tennis players. Because the sisters were so good, they were able to get lessons for free. Instead of going to public school, the girls studied at home so that they could devote more time to tennis. And a lot of time it was! They practiced six hours a day, six days a week. But those

ALTHEA GIBSON

In 1941, when she was 14 years old, Althea Gibson got a present. It was a used tennis racket. Althea had always liked sports. Now she could try a new one. She liked tennis from the start.

Althea lived in Harlem, New York. Most athletic clubs did not allow black people. Althea practiced at a tennis club for African Americans. She entered tournaments for black people and won many of them. Over the next few years, Althea was able to compete in events against white people. But she didn't do very well.

Then, in 1955, she joined a U.S. traveling tennis team. Her game got better. In 1956, she won the French championship. She was the first African American to win a major tournament. In 1957, she played at Wimbledon, the most famous tennis tournament in the world. She won the tournament and became the world's top-ranked player. She helped open up the game for African American players.

Althea Gibson liked sports more than school—especially tennis. As a goodwill ambassador on a traveling team, she developed her game—and proved that black players could play great tennis.

hours were necessary for Venus and Serena to achieve their goal. They wanted to be ranked the number one and number two players in the world.

Dave Rineberg was the girls' hitting coach in the 1990s. He wrote a book called *Venus & Serena: My Seven Years as Hitting Coach for the Williams Sisters*. In it, he says that Venus learned quickly. "If she was unsure about how to hit a shot she would say, 'show me.' I would show her the shot and then she would just do it. It was like she had a built-in computer that processed information and spit it back out through her racquet."

Practicing wasn't all work. They kept things fun, too. Rineberg says that both sisters liked to play jokes. One thing they did was have "Opposite Day." When Rineberg asked for one shot, they gave him another. If he asked for blue Gatorade, they gave him red.

Venus, who was growing taller each day, liked to measure herself against her coach to see if she had outgrown him. Rineberg tricked her. He put extra liners in his shoes to make himself taller. Then one day Venus caught him. She took the joke in good fun, but that was the end of that game.

Richard Williams kept a close eye on things. If he thought practice was getting too stressful, he would cancel it and take the girls to Disney World. He also encouraged them in his own ways. One day at practice, Venus wasn't playing near the net like she should have been. Richard offered to pay her a quarter every time she came to the net. By the end of practice, she'd earned almost $50!

Venus was older, and she was a better player than Serena. Most of the focus was on her. But Serena was paying attention. She worked as hard as Venus, and she was improving, too. After all, the person she played most was Venus.

Despite their grueling practice schedule, both Williams sisters had time to get a good education. Their parents made sure of that. Both of them read a lot of books. They learned to speak French. They brought home A's and B's on their report cards. Their parents didn't allow C's. If they didn't get good grades, they couldn't play tennis.

Neither one of them was willing to risk that.

Chapter Two

THE PATH TO THE TOP

Richard knew tennis was important in his daughters' lives. However, it was not the most important thing. By the time Venus was 14, she was good enough to turn professional. Richard thought that was a bad idea. He didn't want Venus to succeed too early. He thought it would create problems later on. He didn't want a teenaged star who would crash and burn by the time she was in her 20s.

However, just a few months later, Venus did go pro. Richard had said he did not want that. A lot of people were confused when Venus joined the Women's Tennis Association (WTA) in 1994. However, the WTA was getting ready to change its rules. Players would only be allowed to compete in a limited number of tournaments. If Venus joined right away, she would get in before the rules changed. That way she would at least have the option to play.

Venus's professional debut was in Oakland, California, at the Bank of the West Classic. The week before, her coaches urged Richard to have Venus practice more. Instead, Richard took the family on vacation.

Venus entered the tournament unseeded (unranked). She advanced through the first round. In the second, she came up against the top-seeded player Arantxa Sanchez-Vicario. Venus won the first set. She put up a good fight in the second before she finally lost. But she proved the buzz. She was a player to be reckoned with.

Venus was making headlines, but Serena was learning fast. After Venus's debut, Richard stated that Serena had a better feel for the game.

Raw determination shows on Venus's face as she reaches for a shot. She was 14 at her professional debut at the Bank of the West Classic in Oakland, California, in 1994.

She was more aggressive on the court. In short, he said, Serena was better than Venus.

Serena turned pro in 1995. In her first match, she lost to an unremarkable player. The next year she didn't play any professional matches. She lost another tournament in 1997. Was Richard wrong about Serena?

A few months later, Serena played in another tournament. This time she faced Mary Pierce, a top-10 player. Serena won! Next, she played Monica Seles. Seles was ranked fourth. Serena beat Seles, too! Serena eventually lost in the semifinals, but not before she had beaten two top-10 players.

RULES OF THE GAME, SET, MATCH

Tennis is played in three parts. First, comes a game. To win a game, a player must win at least four points and be ahead by two. A group of games makes up a set. A set goes to at least six games. Usually, the winner must be ahead by at least two games to win a set. However, if both players have won six games, they usually play only one more game—a special tiebreaker. In big tournaments, though, the players will have to be ahead by two games in the final match. Finally, a match is made up of a certain number of sets. There are usually five sets in men's tournaments and three in women's. If a woman wins a match in straight sets, it means she won the first two. There is no need to play a third. If it takes all three, then the winning player is said to have won in three sets.

Serena had entered the tournament ranked #304. Afterward, she jumped to #102, more than 200 places. By the year's end, she'd cracked the top 100, coming in at #99. Both sisters were rising fast in the rankings. In 1998, Serena hit #21. Venus claimed the #5 spot.

They hadn't yet reached their goal to be #1 and #2. However, no one doubted that the Williams sisters were serious players.

PLAYING STYLES

Venus Williams has the build of a runner. Before she focused on tennis, she competed in track events. She is tall (6'1", or 185.4 centimeters), fast, and graceful. With her long legs, she can cross the court in only a few strides. With her long arms, she can reach shots that would sail right past shorter players.

Serena is also tall (5'10", or 177.8 cm), but not quite as tall as her sister. Her body looks like a swimmer's. It is compact and muscular. If Venus leaps like a gazelle, Serena crouches and pounces like a mountain lion.

Venus was a little faster; Serena a little stronger. Compared to other women playing tennis, however, both girls were extremely powerful.

Venus in particular became an awesome server. Later in her career, she set the record for the fastest serve by a woman—130 miles per hour (209 kilometers per hour). That's about twice the speed limit on the highway.

One day, Serena was riding her skateboard and wiped out. She hurt her wrist while breaking her fall. She could not hit her backhand while her wrist was healing. But Serena found a way around that problem—literally. When a ball came that needed her backhand, she ran around it. Then she returned it from her forehand position. That was how she built up her forehand shot.

Steadily, the girls developed their games. They worked on their weaknesses until they were no longer weaknesses.

Serena Williams celebrates after beating top player Monica Seles in 1997. She was 16 years of age at the time.

A BUMPY ROAD

The Williams sisters were taking a different path to the top. They did not play at many tournaments. When they did play, they kept to themselves. Some of the other players thought the sisters were unfriendly.

In 1997, Venus played in the semifinals of the U.S. Open. Her opponent was Irina Spirlea, a Romanian woman. The match was a tough fight. During a changeover—when the players switch sides of the court—the two crashed into each other. This incident came to be known in the tennis world as "the bump." Venus tried to downplay what happened, but Irina said something mean about Venus. Over the years, other players made unkind comments about Venus and Serena. One player complained that when she smiled at Venus, Venus didn't smile back.

Richard's behavior also attracted attention. When Venus played at Wimbledon in 2000, Richard was in the stands. He held a sign that said, "It's Venus's party, no one is invited." Some people believed he controlled the girls' games. They said that if the sisters played each other, Richard told them who should win. However, these rumors were never proven.

Richard complained that they endured a lot of racist comments and behavior. But Venus and Serena have not let their race get in their way. Their mother, Oracene, has said, "Yes, they're black, that's pretty obvious. But they realize the person inside matters more than the color of their skin. I think they want to be role models . . . for all kids, not just black kids."

Romanian player Irina Spirlea was defeated by Venus Williams in the match that became famous for "the bump."

Serena *(left)* and Venus Williams were all smiles at the Lipton Tennis Championships in 1999. In the final, Venus beat her sister in three sets. It was the first time they had met each other in a final match.

Venus and Serena looked different on the court, too. They wore beads in their hair. They made fashion statements with their outfits. It seemed the tennis world didn't know what to make of Venus and Serena. But the fans loved their energy and sense of style.

Athletic companies wanted them to endorse their products. If Venus or Serena said this pair of shoes or that tennis racket was the one to use, it could mean a lot of money in sales. Venus signed her first big deal in 1995, with Reebok. It was worth $12 million—and she'd played only one professional tournament!

In 1998, Serena signed a deal with Puma. It was also worth $12 million, as long as Serena became a top-10 player. A little more than a year later, she did.

FAMILY FIRST

Despite the fact that some people didn't like them, Venus and Serena didn't seem to care. They had each other. At major tournaments, each player can have her own hotel room. She can ride in a private car to get to the tennis courts. But Venus and Serena didn't want two of everything. They shared.

In practice, they played each other all the time. They had nicknames for each other. Venus was "Ace." Serena answered to "Smash." But professionally, things were different. They did not want to keep each other from succeeding, so for a long time, they did not enter the same tournaments. However, this strategy would not last forever.

At the 1998 Australian Open, they played each other for the first time as professionals. Later that year, they met at the Italian Open. Venus won both times. So far they hadn't faced each other in the finals, however. They knew that someday they would have to meet each other for the championship.

That came in 1999 at the Lipton Championship, where Venus triumphed over Serena in three sets. In October of that year, the sisters met at another final, the Grand Slam Cup. This time, Serena beat her sister.

Chapter Three

The Ball in Their Court

Serena always wanted to be like Venus. She played tennis because of Venus. She dressed like her older sister. Venus told a reporter her goal was to win Wimbledon. When Serena was asked about her goal, she said the same thing. But then Serena decided to set her own goals. Venus had claimed Wimbledon. Serena set her sights on the U.S. Open.

Many professional tennis tournaments are held each year. The four most important ones are the U.S. Open, the French Open, the Australian Open, and Wimbledon. Together, they are called the Grand Slam. The best professional players compete at Grand Slam tournaments.

In 1999, Serena competed at the U.S. Open. In the finals she played Martina Hingis. Hingis was the number one ranked player in the world. But Serena won! She was the lowest-seeded player ever to win that tournament. Her win was the first Grand Slam title for a Williams sister.

At the time, Serena was ranked below Venus. And of course, since Venus was older, most people thought Venus would win the family's first Grand Slam tournament. But it was not to be. After Serena won, TV cameras showed Venus in the crowd. She looked stunned.

However, Venus soon got another chance to prove herself at a major event. In 2000, she played at Wimbledon.

VENUS MOVES UP

Some tennis matches are played on a hard surface, like clay. Others, like Wimbledon, are played on grass. Venus was an excellent grass player. She liked the soft feel of it under her feet. She didn't mind that the ball didn't bounce as high as it did on a hard court.

The first challenge Venus faced at the 2000 Wimbledon was Serena. They played in the semifinals. Before their match, Venus spoke with the British newspaper the *Independent*. She said, "The biggest challenge is that Serena is extremely powerful and extremely dangerous—and she knows everything I know. That's the trouble with sisters, even when they don't play tennis."

Still, Venus beat Serena. Then she went on to conquer Lindsay Davenport in the finals. Venus had her first Grand Slam win! She was the first African American to win Wimbledon since Althea Gibson.

Number-one-seeded Martina Hingis, nicknamed the "Swiss Miss," lost the U.S. Open to Serena Williams on September 11, 1999.

In 2000, Venus renewed her deal with Reebok. This time it was worth $40 million. That was the most money any female athlete had ever gotten. Venus said, "I had a plan, I worked hard, and I achieved. If you ask me, I'm worth it."

Venus Williams needs every inch of her long legs as she races for a ball delivered by her sister Serena. The sisters matched up at the 2008 Wimbledon finals, where Venus won in straight sets.

That summer, both sisters went to the Olympics. Venus brought home the gold medal in women's singles. Playing together, they won the gold in women's doubles. As a team, Venus and Serena are doubly hard to beat!

Now the world was ready for them to play against each other. People wanted a Williams versus Williams final. And they wanted it at a Grand Slam event. The matchup would come in 2001 at the U.S. Open.

CBS Television was going to broadcast the match. The network knew it would be hugely popular. Even people who didn't usually follow tennis knew about Venus and Serena. More than 20 million people tuned in to see the sister showdown.

Serena was one of the best players in the world. She had won the U.S. Open two years earlier. But this time, Serena didn't get the prize. In their first final at a Grand Slam event, Venus came out on top.

THE SISTER SLAMS

In 2002, the sisters reached the goal they had set for themselves years ago. In February, Venus reached the very top. She was ranked the number one female player in the world. Three months later, Serena moved up to number two, just under her sister. She wouldn't stay there for long.

When the two sisters met in the finals of a Grand Slam event, the media called the event

THE PRESIDENT IS CALLING

After Venus won the U.S. Open in 2001, President Bill Clinton called to congratulate her. Many people would be nervous if they got a call from the president of the United States. They might manage to stammer out "Thank you, sir" before hanging up. Not Venus. She had plenty to say.

First, she asked the president why he had left the tournament before her match. Then she complained that his motorcade caused a traffic jam. She got stuck in it. Next she wanted to know if he could do anything about the high taxes she had to pay. The people listening to the phone call were surprised at all the things she said. Venus didn't think it was a big deal. "I'm not really intimidated by anyone," she said. "Why should I be?"

a Sister Slam. The spring of 2002 would start a string of Sister Slams that lasted for eight months.

In June, they played each other at the finals of the French Open. Serena won. She added a Wimbledon win against her sister in July. That win also marked another milestone for Serena. That was when she knocked Venus out of the number one spot.

Then Serena beat Venus in the finals of the U.S. Open in September. January 2003 brought her face-to-face with Venus at the Australian Open finals. When Serena won that championship, it meant that she had won all four Grand Slam tournaments in a row.

Serena was now the reigning champion for all four events. However, she could not say that she held the title of Grand Slam winner. Why not? The rules of tennis stated that all four events had to be won in the same calendar year. Serena's win at the Australian Open was in 2003, not 2002. Serena didn't let it bother her. She just called her achievement the "Serena Slam."

Serena told *Tennis* magazine, "To finally win a match against Venus in a big tournament was a pretty big confidence booster. I learned that it's OK to do well against your sister."

What about Venus? "I want to win," she told the magazine. "But I want [Serena] to win also, because . . . basically I want the best for her." She added, "My goal has always been to be No. 1 in the world. But not to take the No. 1 ranking from my sister."

Venus and Serena were ranked in the top handful of tennis players in the world. In 2003, they received an award at the NAACP Image Awards, which recognizes the contributions of black people. Then NAACP president Kweisi Mfume said, "They are prime examples that there is no substitute for brains, hard work, and dedication."

The Williams sisters show their patriotism after taking the gold medal for women's doubles at the 2000 Olympics in Sydney, Australia.

To win tournaments, other players knew they would have to beat Venus, or Serena, or both. The name "Williams" was everywhere. It seemed like it would be that way for a long time.

SETBACKS

Soon, however, the sisters began to have some problems. In 2002, their parents divorced. Then in 2003, tragedy struck. Yetunde Price, their oldest sister, was shot to death in their old neighborhood of Compton. Both sisters said that Yetunde was a huge source of strength to them. They were devastated by her death.

Another problem was injuries. Professional athletes stay in great shape. They are stronger and more flexible than most people. But they ask a lot of their bodies. Most people don't get injured when they play a casual game

Chris Evert, a talented and well-liked tennis player, helped make women's tennis a popular game. Later she went to work for *Tennis* magazine, where she kept a close eye on the careers of the Williams sisters.

of tennis on a Saturday morning. Then again, most people do not hit the ball more than 100 mph (160 km per hour)! Professional athletes often get hurt. Sometimes, it can keep them away from the game for months.

Serena won Wimbledon again in 2003, but then she hurt her knee. She could not play as much. She lost the number one ranking she had held for more than a year. Throughout 2004, 2005, and 2006, she suffered other injuries.

Venus also struggled with keeping her body healthy. She injured her wrist, her ankle, and a muscle around her stomach. Even though they were not playing tennis, both sisters kept busy with other projects. Some people wondered if they were abandoning the game.

Chris Evert was a tennis superstar in the 1970s and 1980s. Later she went to work for *Tennis* magazine. In June 2006, Evert wrote a letter to Serena in the magazine. Serena was considered the better player at this point. Evert asked Serena why she did not focus on tennis.

"Dear Serena," the letter read, "I appreciate that becoming a well-rounded person is important to you, as you've made that desire very clear. Still . . . Do you ever consider your place in history? . . . In the short term you may be happy with the various things going on in your life, but I wonder whether 20 years from now you might reflect on your career and regret not putting 100 percent of yourself into tennis."

Serena responded a few months later in an interview with the magazine. "I learned that you have to do what makes you happy," she said. Whatever other people thought, both sisters knew that tennis was only one part of their lives.

Chapter Four

NEW DIRECTIONS

Venus and Serena were not playing as much tennis as they had a few years earlier. But they had still been busy!

Both of them enjoyed fashion. They showed their style on the court. Serena liked to wear clothes that grabbed people's attention. One year she wore a formfitting outfit that she called "the cat suit." Another time she wore "tennis boots" during her warm-up. (The boots were actually removable pieces that wrapped around her legs.) Once she played while wearing a short, white trench coat. Angela Haynes, another tennis pro from Compton, talked about Serena's look in the book *Charging the Net*. "She's got such a sense of style to her game and her fashion. That's exciting. The fans want to see that. Even people who don't care about tennis are interested in what Serena is wearing."

Serena decided it was time to put her fashion sense to work. In 2004, she started her own fashion line, named Aneres ("Serena" spelled backward). Venus also started her own fashion line. Hers is called EleVen.

Venus and Serena are famous. It would be easy to let someone else design the clothes and then just put their names on them. But neither one of them likes the easy route! When they weren't playing tennis, both of them attended fashion school. They learned how to do the work themselves.

Serena's fashion sense makes an impression along with her tennis. Her famous "tennis boots" were not typical tennis attire, but they did not slow her down on the court.

OTHER PROJECTS

Besides fashion, both sisters are involved in lots of other projects. They will have plenty to do after they retire from tennis. Serena likes to act. She has been on several television shows, like *ER* and *Law and Order: Special Victims Unit*. Venus runs her own interior design business. It is called V Starr Interiors. (Venus's middle name is Ebony Starr.) Even with her hectic practice schedule, Venus tries to spend a few hours each day at the office.

Both sisters are passionate about education. Actually, the whole family is passionate about education. Venus and Serena are impressed by their older sister, Isha. She has four college degrees! Serena wanted to give other people the opportunity to go to school. In 2008, she helped open a school in Kenya, a country in Africa. The school is named after her.

In addition, Venus and Serena hope to give other children a chance to play tennis. They started a tennis academy in Los Angeles, California. Tennis pros give lessons there, and promising players can earn college scholarships. Venus and Serena believe that people should be well rounded. So children who go to the school do other things, too. They visit museums, go to the movies, and even get in some time to study!

Venus and Serena have also written two books together. *How to Play Tennis* helps young tennis

Serena talks with students at the Serena Williams Secondary School in Kenya. Serena helped start the school to bring educational opportunities to African children.

players develop their game. *Venus and Serena: Serving from the Hip* gives girls tips on how to live a balanced and successful life.

BACK IN THE GAME

Wimbledon had always been Venus's dream. She won her first Wimbledon tournament in 2000. She defended her title in 2001. In 2002 and 2003, she lost to Serena. Then, in 2004, Venus was injured and couldn't compete.

Venus had suffered injuries and setbacks. She didn't play that often. She didn't play that well. When she got to Wimbledon in 2005, she was no longer the number one player in the world. She wasn't even in the top 10.

Still, Venus was considered the best grass player of her generation. By 2005, her body had healed. The strong tennis player of a few years earlier had returned. Venus was back where she belonged, on the grass at Wimbledon.

Round by round, Venus moved up—all the way to the finals. There, she faced her rival, Lindsay Davenport. Davenport was ranked number one. The two women played hard for almost three hours. It was the longest women's match in Wimbledon history. First, one woman would pull ahead. Then the other woman would come back. In the third set, Venus was down match point. Davenport was only one good hit away from winning. But Venus did not give up. She had skill and stamina. She fought back and won.

In fact, Wimbledon seems like Venus's favorite place to win. There were nine Wimbledon tournaments between 2000 and 2008. Venus reached the finals seven times. She won five of those.

By the beginning of 2007, Serena was barely ranked in the top 100. However, she said she would be the number one player again. Not everyone agreed. Many people thought Serena had slipped too far to come back. But Serena won two singles titles in 2007, including the Australian Open. In 2008, she was back at the U.S. Open. It had been almost a decade since

SEEING THE LIGHT

Serena learned early how to play tennis. But learning how to be responsible took a little longer! When Serena turned 18, she and Venus decided to move out of their parents' home. They found a house several miles away. Serena told *O, the Oprah Magazine*, that she was ready to be an adult. "[I was] ready to go to bed when I wanted, ready to watch what I wanted on television when I wanted to, ready to hang out with friends and not be asked, 'Serena, where are you going?'"

Then one day Serena got home from a tournament. The electricity had been turned off! She had forgotten to pay the bill. "I was constantly running out of groceries, toiletries, and little things I needed. That's when you realize what it means to be an adult: when you're on your own and you run out of toilet paper."

she had first won. Once again, Serena walked away with the title. With that win, she also did what she had predicted. She took back her spot as the world's number one player.

LEGACY TO TENNIS

Venus and Serena will eventually retire from tennis. However, the sport will always feel their influence. Venus made sure of that.

In 1968, professional tennis switched to what is called the Open Era. This was when players started to win prize money when they won a competition. Despite this step forward, however, there was still a problem. At least, Venus Williams thought it was a problem.

Venus's smile is big, the trophy bigger, and the prize money biggest of all. She won at Wimbledon in 2007 and became the first woman to receive the same amount of money as the men's champion.

Competing at Wimbledon is a huge achievement for a tennis player. However, until only a few years ago, the winner of the men's division got paid more than the winner of the women's division. Venus thought this was unfair.

In 2006, she wrote a letter to the London newspaper *The Times*. "The message I like to convey to women and girls across the globe is that there is no glass ceiling," she wrote. "My fear is that Wimbledon is loudly and clearly sending the opposite message . . ."

Tony Blair was the prime minister of England at the time. He publicly agreed with her. The Women's Tennis Association also supported Venus.

The next year, officials at Wimbledon changed their policy. For the first time in the tournament's history, women would make the same amount as men. The French Open also agreed to pay winners equally.

In 2007, Venus became the first woman to benefit from this change. She won the women's singles title at Wimbledon. Roger Federer won the men's division. They both received equal amounts of money. It was a double victory for Venus.

When Venus and Serena started out in Compton, few people believed they could succeed at tennis. They did that and more. In *Charging the Net*, tennis player James Blake says, "The Williams sisters will definitely leave a footprint. [They] played tennis and made it cool."

In 2006, Serena agreed. She told *Tennis* magazine, "They'll always remember Venus and me for starting a whole new legacy in tennis and a whole new style . . . The physical fitness, the running, the serve, the return, the fashion. We changed the whole game."

Tennis fans will not soon forget Venus and Serena Williams. They brought forceful playing and a daring personal style. They brought a new level of athleticism to the game of tennis. They competed with the best players in the world—including each other. They are rivals and best friends.

Above all, they are sisters.

TIMELINE

1980:

Venus Williams is born.

1981:

Serena Williams is born.

1991:

The Williams family moves to Florida.

1994:

Venus turns pro and plays her first pro match in California.

1995:

Serena turns pro. Venus signs a $12 million deal with Reebok.

1997:

Serena beats two top-10 players and moves into the top 100 players. Venus competes at the U.S. Open.

1998:

Serena signs a $12 million deal with Puma.

1999:

Serena wins the U.S. Open.

2000:

Venus wins Wimbledon and the U.S. Open. Venus renews her deal with Reebok for $40 million. Both sisters compete at the Olympics, where they win a gold medal in doubles and Venus wins the gold in singles.

2001:

The sisters meet at the U.S. Open finals. Venus wins.

2002:

Venus becomes the number one ranked player and Serena moves to number two. Later Serena wins the French Open, Wimbledon, and the U.S. Open and becomes the number one ranked player.

2003:

Serena wins the Australian Open and completes the "Serena Slam." The sisters receive an NAACP Image Award. Older sister Yetunde Price is killed.

2005:

Venus wins Wimbledon in the longest women's match in the tournament's history.

2007:

Venus becomes the first woman to receive prize money equal to men at Wimbledon.

2008:

Venus beats Serena at Wimbledon finals. Serena wins U.S. Open and regains number one ranking. Serena starts a school in Kenya.

2009:

Serena wins her fourth Australian Open. Venus wins the WTA Acapulco Open.

GLOSSARY

academy A school.

ace A tennis serve that cannot be returned.

aggressive Forceful.

benefit To receive something good because of someone's actions.

broadcast To put a program on television.

contribution A way that someone has helped another person or cause.

glass ceiling A term referring to when people can see above them but cannot move there, usually referring to advancing in a career.

heritage The background and history of a group of people.

legacy The long-term influence and contributions that a person or group of people leaves.

match point When the leading player is one point away from winning the match.

motorcade A group of cars carrying an important person and the people who travel with him or her.

opponent The person a player competes against.

renew To extend the time that something is happening.

retire To stop working at a career.

rival A person who is in close competition with another for the same thing.

seed Where a player is ranked entering a tournament.

serve The first shot a tennis player makes to put the ball into play.

smash An overhead tennis shot hit so hard that it is very difficult to return.

stamina The physical ability someone has to keep going, even though he or she is tired.

substitute Something that takes the place of something else.

tournament An event where several rounds of competition are played to determine a winner.

FOR MORE INFORMATION

Althea Gibson Foundation

320 S. Harrison Street, Suite 3C

East Orange, NJ 07018

(973) 672-2088

E-mail: AgibsonFoundation@aol.com

Web site: http://www.altheagibson.com

The organization was formed to help urban youth interested in tennis or golf, and to provide information about Althea Gibson.

American Tennis Association (ATA)

1100 Mercantile Lane, Suite 115A

Largo, MD 20774

(301) 583-4631

E-mail: info@atanational.com

Web site: http://www.atanational.com

The ATA works to promote the involvement of African Americans in the sport of tennis. Formed in 1916, it is the country's oldest African American sports organization.

Tennis Canada

Uniprix Stadium

285 Faillon West

Montreal, QB H2R 2W1

Canada

(514) 273-1515

(866) 338-2685

E-mail: info@tenniscanada.com

Web site: http://www.tenniscanada.com

Tennis Canada is made up of several different tennis organizations in Canada. It works to promote participation and excellence in the sport.

U.S. Professional Tennis Association (USPTA)

3535 Briarpark Drive, Suite One

Houston, TX 77042

(713) 978-7782

(800) USPTA-4U (877-8248)

E-mail: uspta@uspta.org

Web site: http://www.uspta.org

The USPTA is the world's largest and oldest group of professional tennis teachers. It works to improve standards and encourage participation in the sport.

U.S. Tennis Association (USTA)

70 West Red Oak Lane

White Plains, NY 10604

(914) 696-7000

E-mail: usopenwebinfo@usta.com

Web site: http://www.usta.com

The USTA works to promote and develop the sport of tennis at both the professional and amateur levels. It sponsors the U.S. Open.

Venus and Serena Williams Tutorial/Tennis Academy

(California Tennis Association for Underprivileged Youths)

3870 Crenshaw Boulevard, Suite 104

Los Angeles, CA 90008

(323) 292-6844

E-mail: info@venusserenatennisacademy.org

Web site: http://www.venusserenatennisacademy.org

The Williams sisters' tennis academy offers tennis lessons and educational support, and helps players gain scholarships.

Women's Tennis Association (WTA)

Corporate Headquarters

One Progress Plaza, Suite 1500

St. Petersburg, FL 33701

(727) 895-5000

Web site: http://www.sonyericssonwtatour.com

The WTA sponsors tournaments throughout the year for professional women tennis players.

World Team Tennis (WTT)

1776 Broadway, Suite 600

New York, NY 10019

(212) 586-3444

E-mail: customerservice@wtt.com

Web site: http://www.worldteamtennis.com

The WTT sponsors coed professional teams and promotes recreational play. Children can participate in several programs.

WEB SITES

Due to the changing nature of Internet links, Rosen Publishing has developed an online list of Web sites related to the subject of this book. This site is updated regularly. Please use this link to access the list:

http://www.rosenlinks.com/sfam/will

FOR FURTHER READING

Berman, Ron. *The Kid from Courage*. La Jolla, CA: Scobre Press, 2003.

Clippinger, Carol. *Open Court*. New York, NY: Knopf Books for Young Readers, 2007.

Edmondson, Jacqueline. *Venus and Serena Williams: A Biography*. Westport, CT: Greenwood Press, 2005.

Feinstein, John. *Vanishing Act: Mystery at the U.S. Open*. New York, NY: Knopf Books for Young Readers, 2006.

Fillon, Mike. *Young Superstars of Tennis: The Venus and Serena Williams Story*. Greensboro, NC: Avisson Press, Inc., 1999.

Gormley, Beatrice. *Althea Gibson: Young Tennis Player*. New York, NY: Aladdin, 2005.

Marcovitz, Hal. *Venus and Serena Williams*. Broomall, PA: Mason Crest Publishers, 2008.

Porter, David. *Winning Tennis for Girls*. New York, NY: Facts On File, 2003.

Rineberg, Dave. *Venus & Serena: My Seven Years as Hitting Coach for the Williams Sisters*. Hollywood, FL: Frederick Fell Publishers, Inc., 2003.

Todd, Anne M. *Venus and Serena Williams*. New York, NY: Chelsea House, 2009.

Williams, Venus, and Serena Williams. *How to Play Tennis*. New York, NY: DK Publishing, 2004.

Williams, Venus, and Serena Williams, with Hilary Beard. *Venus and Serena: Serving from the Hip*. New York, NY: Houghton Mifflin Company, 2005.

BIBLIOGRAPHY

Edmondson, Jacqueline. *Venus and Serena Williams: A Biography*. Westport, CT: Greenwood Press, 2005.

Evert, Chris. "Dear Serena." *Tennis*, May 2006, p. 12.

Fillon, Mike. *Young Superstars of Tennis: The Venus and Serena Williams Story*. Greensboro, NC: Avisson Press, Inc., 1999.

Flatman, Barry. "Venus and Serena Williams Silence Critics." *The Times*, July 6, 2008. Retrieved December 2, 2008 (http://www.timesonline.co.uk/tol/sport/tennis/article4276540.ece).

Harris, Cecil, and Larryette Kyle-DeBose. *Charging the Net: A History of Blacks in Tennis from Althea Gibson and Arthur Ashe to the Williams Sisters*. Chicago, IL: Ivan R. Dee, 2007.

King, Dale. "Are Venus and Serena Williams Supernovas?" AmericanChronicle.com, August 13, 2006. Retrieved December 2, 2008 (http://www.americanchronicle.com/articles/view/12444).

Lamb, Yanick Rice. "Sister Act: Venus and Serena Williams Set the Rules in a New Book of Advice for Young Women." *Black Issues Book Review*, September/October 2005. Retrieved December 2, 2008 (http://findarticles.com/p/articles/mi_m0HST/is_5_7/ai_n15763620).

Lister, David. "Venus and Serena Williams Win Place in Tennis History." *The Independent*, July 5, 2000. Retrieved December 2, 2008 (http://www.independent.co.uk/sport/tennis/venus-and-serena-williams-win-place-in-tennis-history-709250.html).

Martin, James. "The Surreal Life of Serena Williams." *Tennis*, October 2006, pp. 40–42.

Oprah.com. "Tennis Star Venus Williams." Retrieved December 2, 2008 (http://www.oprah.com/article/oprahandfriends/gking/gking_20071116).

Park, Michael Y. "Venus Williams: Serena Is Key to My Success." People.com, July 7, 2008. Retrieved December 15, 2008 (http://www.people.com/people/article/0,,20210714,00.html?xid=rss-fullcontentcnn).

Rineberg, Dave. *Venus & Serena: My Seven Years as Hitting Coach for the Williams Sisters*. Hollywood, FL: Frederick Fell Publishers, Inc., 2003.

Roberts, Selena. "TENNIS; Venus Williams Wins Wimbledon, Lighting Up Center Court." *New York Times*, July 9, 2000. Retrieved December 16,

2008 (http://query.nytimes.com/gst/fullpage.html?res = 9E0CE4DB1538F93AA35754C0A9669C8B63&sec = &spon = &pagewanted = all).

Schoenfeld, Bruce. "The Venus Trap." *Tennis*, July 2003, pp. 40–46.

Sports Illustrated. "*Sports Illustrated* Scrapbook: Venus and Serena Williams." Retrieved December 2, 2008 (http://sportsillustrated.cnn.com/tennis/features/williams/main).

Stein, Joel. "The Power Game." *Time*, September 3, 2001. Retrieved November 24, 2008 (http://www.time.com/time/magazine/article/0,9171,1000673,00.html).

Thomas, Devon, and Tom Cunneff. "Celeb Spotlight: Venus & Serena Williams." People.com, July 21, 2005. Retrieved December 2, 2008 (http://www.people.com/people/article/0,,1084996,00.html).

VoiceOfAmerica.com. "Sister of U.S. Tennis Stars Venus and Serena Williams Killed." September 15, 2003. Retrieved December 15, 2008 (http://www.voanews.com/english/archive/2003-09/a-2003-09-15-24-Sister.cfm).

Wertheim, L. Jon. *Venus Envy*. New York, NY: HarperCollins Publishers, Inc., 2001.

Williams, Serena, as told to David Thorpe. "Serena Williams's Aha! Moment." *O, the Oprah Magazine*, January 2008, p. 69.

ABOUT THE AUTHOR

Diane Bailey grew up in the 1970s, when tennis was all the rage. She remembers spending many hours at the local tennis court with her family—mostly fetching balls! She has two children and writes on a variety of nonfiction topics.

PHOTO CREDITS